THE CALL OF MOTHER EARTH

HOW A BEING OF LIGHT DRAWS FORTH HUMANITY'S RESPONSE

Verse Narrative and Artwork by

Clare Rosenfield

Published by Gatekeeper Press
2167 Stringtown Rd, Suite 109
Columbus, OH 43123-2989
www.GatekeeperPress.com

Copyright © 2004-2021 by Clare S. Rosenfield

All rights reserved. No part of this publication may be reproduced, distributed, stored in a retrieval system, or transmitted in any form or by any means, electronic, mechanical, photocopying, recording, or otherwise, without the prior written permission of the author, except in the case of brief quotations embodied in critical reviews and certain other noncommercial uses permitted by copyright law.

For permission requests or quantity sales, contact
Clare Rosenfield at **crosenfield9@gmail.com**.

Library of Congress Control Number 2017908712
ISBN 9781662919466

Printed in the United States of America

DEDICATION

To the one mother of us all, Gaia, our Earthmother,

that she may feel loved, respected, and cherished,

that she may be restored to her natural state of abundance,

generosity, and perfect health,

that her wisdom may be heard and honored,

that human beings cease to cause her and themselves

further suffering

and instead partner with her in the great work of Awakening,

in the recognition that how lovingly we relate to Gaia,

the body of our body,

our planetary home,

is how truly we care for ourselves.

May the healing arising from this poetic narrative be a blessing

for generations to come.

APPRECIATION

In appreciation of the living legacy that Sufi masters Hazrat Inayat Khan and Pir Vilayat Khan, his son, brought to the West in the form of the Message of Love, Harmony, and Beauty, known as the "Universel", an inner temple or template for creating a new and conscious humanity, one that honors the wisdom-teachings from all paths in a Universal Worship or Cosmic Celebration and leads Universal Dances for Peace drawn from many diverse backgrounds.

In appreciation of the Abode of the Message, its sacred mountains, organic farm, retreat huts, meditation hall, and all that it offers to sincere seekers of experiential truth as well as to children.

In appreciation of Aziza Scott for bringing me in closer touch with the Divine Feminine.

In appreciation of Amritanandamayima, known as Ammachi, for being a living Mother Earth to those whom she embraces and who embrace her worldwide.

In appreciation of the late Jacques Tombazian for helping me discover a deeper connection to Gaia, our Earthmother, and to realize the transformative healing power of a pure intention.

In appreciation of Joy Stephan who began the formatting process and of the late Marite B. Jones who brought it to completion, adding to it the perfect artistic touch and her infinite patience with the computer.

In appreciation of Ann Weiner and Lilly Langotsky for their artistic advice and of Lindsay Birch for her continued encouragement and upbeat technical assistance.

PREFACE

I have fallen in love with larger-than-life beings. Beings of Light are as real to me as they are necessary in this critical dot in historical time. They abide not only in my imagination, but also in the living reality of what inspires my heart. Monk-like and contemplative most of my life, I have come in touch with some wellsprings within.

Longings to know what is true and real. Cries for solace and intimacy, the kind of soul resonance which can reveal itself to another in complete openness and innocence because it is unthreatened and safe. These represent two poles—the pull which takes me to my depths, in solitude, and the push which propels me to offer something of value to others, in communication.

The theme of the Call and the Response has reverberated in me all my life. Whenever a biblical figure responds to God with the wholehearted words, "Here I am," I am moved. I too want to bring forth the goddess, the prophetess, the being of Light in myself, and let my heart respond fully, then my hands.

I have great hopes for humankind. This prose poem gives a blueprint for humanity. We can access the archetypal dimensions in ourselves. We can hear the plaintive call of our Earthmother. We can respond in our own way. Together we can feel into the Heart of the universe; we can think with Higher Mind.

Until now, if we have been learning about the threats to our environment, our soil, the rainforests, the icecaps, our climate, our waterways, we have been scaring ourselves and perhaps feeling powerless. Now it is time to inspire ourselves and extol the beauties and capacities of Mother Nature, and in so doing, lift ourselves to a vision that can heal her, as it heals us all.

It is my secret longing that someone will turn this story with its series of poetic dialogues into a musical play or operetta, so that its message can be heard as song and drama, and reverberate from earth to sky, in all of space.

CALLS AND RESPONSES

THE CALL   1

KA-ELA'S ARRIVAL 7

KA-ELA SPEAKS TO THE VILLAGERS   11

INVOKING MOTHER EARTH   17

KA-ELA'S INVITATION   30

EARTHMOTHER'S MESSAGE   33

BECOMING A COSMIC BEING   41

COSMIC EMBODIMENT   46

CONSCIOUS ATTUNEMENT   51

DREAM-HEALING 56

AWAKENING TO DAWN 58

HIGH NOONTIME 63

KA-ELA'S DEPARTURE   66

THE CALL

And a being of Light
was bathing in sunbeams and splendor
when she felt as if stabbed
hearing from afar agony and groans.

"Who could this be?" she thought to herSelf.

It was Mother Earth,
plundered and at her wit's end, crying out,

"Please O beings of Light!
Whoever hears my plea,
come, I implore you,
please put on a body and descend.
Only an illuminated being can create the miracle
which will transform this world."

The being of Light dropped deep into herSelf

and let her innermost listen and feel.
She lived as a witness to the heavens,
in the light of innocence and peace.
She resonated with the happiness
of the angelic.
Now she heard a new calling—
to answer the need of Earthmother
and all her earthling children
for a transformative light,
for inspiration and rededication
to ideals,
lived ideals,
illumined thoughts embodied
in enlightened action.

And so she uttered her response
by telepathy,

"Yes, I will heed your moans, O Earthmother.
I will fashion an earth-body,
infuse it with rays of light,
and fly to a mountaintop
at the height of your planet,
and from there I will speak
and be heard."

"O, thank you, dear angelic one,

for I have been pillaged and plundered,
raped to the core.
Always I believed in my powers
to regenerate and renew dying life.
I gave every resource I had
and all manner of fruit and of seed,
but now with pollution,
and minds bent on profit,
there's no turning back.
I cannot do my work,
my service, my surrender,
my gift.
I am broken of heart
and need to reach out to
voices of love and of reason.
Yet I've lost my voice
and all I do
is quake and bring flood
and destruction.
I don't mean to,
but the laws of my life
are speaking this way
for survival.
I'm pleading with you,
please speak in a language
they can hear."

"Say no more, Mother Earth,
I have fashioned myself
into human form,
woven thicker layers of light
until they have become solid yet airy,
concentrated yet spacious.

"I am ready and flying.
Soon I shall reach your shores.
Call out to me
anytime you wish.
I shall hear you from deep within.
My abode will be high on a mountain
and from there I will speak.
Do you hear me?"

"O I hear you and
thank you, my friend from on high,
my friend who will bring me back to myself
and with me, humanity back to its senses.
Tell me,
do you have a name?
I should like to know how to call you."

"I have no name for I am all names,

truth and all wisdom and love.
I am mastery and mystery,
majesty and splendor.
I am gatherer and disperser
of energies of all kinds.
I inspire and sing and dance and shout,
out of ecstasy pour forth
great blessings,
but as a new human,
I shall take on a name.
You can call me Ka-Ela."

"How beautiful, my friend,
Ka-Ela you are,
and Ka-Ela shall you ever be.
I surrender to that
which I know you will do
to rescue this world and restore
wholeness to creation.
And now I shall rest
and lay down for a while
the struggles to right
all the wrongs.
I leave all to you
and await the hour you will tell me
the healing's begun."

"Rest, Mother Earth,
rest all your limbs,
from your heights to your depths,
rest from your burdens and plight."

KA-ELA'S ARRIVAL

After this grand dialogue took place,
Ka-Ela flew down,
adorned with a raiment of celestial light.
A rainbow cloud accompanied her and
landed with her upon the mountain.
Soon at its base
where a village lay nestled,
some villagers noticed that rainbow
and an unearthly light.

Word passed quickly from one to the other
that some miraculous cloud
with a rainbow-like aura
had been sighted atop their mountain.
And that very night,
as they all looked up from their huts,
they saw on this night of no moon
an unusual emission of radiance and color,

and believed that a god had descended.

No one dared go and see who he or she was
but a lone climber of peaks.
When he offered to go,
the people said,

"You have no idea what
will happen. Don't go!"

The young man whose name was Eli said,

"No, I am not in the least afraid.
What is unknown can offer me beauty.
What is unknown can reveal to me mystery.
What is unknown can teach me a teaching."

And off he went on a seven-day hike
to the peak of the peak
of the peak.

Just as he was about to reach the summit,
he slipped, and nearly dropped into a crevice
deep in a ravine.
At that last moment, a hand scooped him up,
a soft, gentle hand,
and he looked up and saw,
to his joy and surprise,

a goddess-like being,
Ka-Ela.

"O, thank you, angelic woman,
for saving my life!
Who are you and why
have you come here?"

"I have come from the great beyond.
I am here as a soothing healing presence
in this world.
I come to the rescue of Earthmother
in her plight."

"O," exclaimed Eli, "you are a prophetess,
a goddess.
How can I help you?
I love Mother Earth
and have used a lot of my life
to get to know her."

"What is your name, young man?"

"Eli, O angelic being, and what is yours?"

"Ka-Ela."

"Ah," he responded. "And what does that name mean?"

"You will know in time.
For now, here is how
you can help. Tell your fellow villagers to gather
themselves together and I will descend to a
midway point on this mountain. Let them bring me
their open hearts and questioning minds."

"Ka-Ela, most of them have frightened hearts
and doubting minds."

"Never mind. None of that is lasting.
They will have a change of heart soon."

KA-ELA SPEAKS TO THE VILLAGERS

Eli gathered the villagers and guided them to the midway point
of the mountain where the radiant Ka-Ela greeted them
joyfully.

"Welcome! My friends! You may think it odd
that I call you my friends, but I speak of
your beautiful hearts and souls,
the invisible blueprint within your bodies,
the reason you came to earth."

One villager named Nikos asked,

"What do you mean by a blueprint?
Is there a code in each of us
we have no knowledge of? Is that
the reason we are here?"

"Yes, exactly. Each of us has a true core,

a treasury of knowledge,

an inner abode,

and a mandate to express it, and

all the talents we need to

bring it out in our own unique ways."

Another villager named Helena commented,

"Is it different for each person?"

"Each person has different angles of vision
and expressive voices to bring the knowledge
out into the light of day."

A third villager named Maitri asked,

"How are we to access that knowledge?"

Ka-Ela explained,

"There is one basic premise and it is this —
The world we live in is a garden of love,
of harmony, of beauty in its original, non-tampered state.
Before human beings uprooted the trees and paved
over the earth and carved into our Earthmother,
this place was a perfect mirror of our inner garden."

"Our inner garden?"

"Yes, our inner garden is a state of nature. It is
perfect and complete. There is nothing you cannot
find there. It is when you feel cut off from these roots,
this garden, this inner abode,
that you miss seeing and feeling your beauty.
All you need to do is stop, look, sense
what you carry within you —
a vast treasury, a reservoir of knowledge,
lovingkindness and harmony."

"Look and sense into what?"

"Let your eyes rest on the shelf of space,
let your breathing go quiet and natural
under the canopy of your loving watchful inner eye.
Let your body feel the support of the ground,
of your Earthmother,
and sense deeply your original innocence,
your state of nature."

Nikos admitted,

"But we are not

innocent. We have gambled and raged,
we have deceived and lied about our actions.
We have not always lived in a state of
mutual love, harmony, or nature."

Ka-Ela answered,

"Of course, I know that
and I appreciate your honesty.
But that is only a partial truth.
You are not aware of your innocent state of nature
because you have missed
the main truth— this vast resource
inside yourself. You have not realized
that it exists. Once you value it,
you can ask it to teach you
what you long to know. Then you will regain
your original state and
access to the infinite wisdom of the
universe.

"And you will learn
how to take care of your planetary home,
the gifts of your Earthmother."

Eli called out,

"Could you please speak to us of our Earthmother
and how it is that you are here among us."

"Gladly! Now hear this," began Ka-Ela.

"Our Earthmother is falling apart.
She has a broken heart.
and feels violated, plundered, robbed
of her treasures, her purpose.
She has always been here to provide, nourish,
renew, and now she feels spent,
unable to fulfill her greatest joy.
I heard her moans, her sobs,
and responded to her request."

"What was that, O great being?"

"To leave my diaphanous soul state
and don a human body, descend to
your planet and become a co-creatrice
with you for the sake of our Earthmother
and all of this universe of life."

A great sigh passed through the crowd.

"This being in our midst is
a goddess, an angel in human garb,
a prophetess.

"Let us listen carefully to her and
"awaken to what we can do to be of help,
each of us, separately and together."

"Yes, yes, yes," was heard throughout
the huddled group of barely ninety-nine persons.

INVOKING MOTHER EARTH

Ka-Ela suggested,

"Let us invoke our Earthmother
and ask her in our own personal voices
to speak to us. Are you willing?"

"How?" Helena asked.

"Just let your gaze soften and rest,
or perhaps close your eyes ever so gently
so that you barely feel the lids touching.
Now sense into the weight of your limbs,
arms and legs, hands and feet, your spinal column,
and acknowledge that it is thanks to
the earth element that you have a body
and a connection to gravity and balance
and support.

"After that, awaken to your natural inhalation
and exhalation without making any effort
to disturb it or change it.
Let that natural breath be in the backdrop
of your mind just like a rhythm
behind a piece of music.

"Let most of your mind open like a vast window
to the spacious space all around you and
within you
and let that space feel receptive, silent, dark or luminous.

"Then, you will know what you have to say
to Mother Earth.
And when you do, speak from your heart's longing.
Speak it silently or in a whisper or out loud,
as you wish, and then touch into the silence.
Be receptive to what she has to say back to you.
All right? Let us begin, each one, in our own way."

From the many hearts assembled there,
at the midway point of the special mountain,
in a sunny clearing surrounded by tall grasses
and low-growing berry bushes,
here are the prayers and invocations
that Mother Earth heard and

here is the love and compassion she received
into the heart of her soul,
as a balm to heal her sorrow
and wounding.

One by one, prayers were uttered,
each in different vocabulary,
each with deep-rooted sincerity.

The first prayer came from Eli,

"O Mother Earth,
I feel for your pain.
I am coming to realize that we humans are
only skin deep.
Whatever part is touching you,
the soles of our feet or the base of our spines
is only a tiny portion of us
contacting a tiny portion of you.
We are made of you
and wrapped up in your earthenware,
but we touch only the edge of your skin,
while we wrangle over the ownership of you,
as if we believe in the illusion
that mere patches of land
belong to us.

"How could we do this?
Those patches are just skin deep.
Way down to the heart and core of you
we cannot reach,
yet, I shudder, some have even exploded bombs
into your body.
How can any of us think we own you?
Even one patch of you?

"Forgive us, O Earthmother of ours,
you have the right to an intact body,
to a wholeness which has ever been
the source of your capacity to nourish and
give to us.
May you be ready once again
to offer those gifts for germinating life,
for recycling atoms,
for creating conditions favorable
for burgeoning and blooming."

Upon hearing Eli's words,
Mother Earth shivered and shook,
for even though she felt understood,
she did not have the energy
to utter a word in response.

Then Maitri addressed his
thoughts in this way,

"Dear Mother Earth,
mankind is myopic.
We assert our false identity
as dominant and superior
by exploding, raping, destroying
our mother.
O my God, no wonder you are
reeling with dis-ease.
Blown apart, you can no longer
find a way to give.
Your resources are dried up.
Without you, we cannot live.
Starvation. No grain, no trees, no fruit,
no vegetation.
O generous-hearted one, our planetary guardian,
you weep inconsolably.
I weep with you.
Please be renewed by my love,
by our collective love."

And tears came from Earthmother,
and everyone wept with her.

And still another villager named Aura whispered,
"O motherly Earth,
how could I have forgotten
to appreciate you and all the nourishing
of seeds that you do as your primary work?
And O the multifarious manifestations of you,
earth-rooted one,
the exquisiteness of seeds
turning into shoots and stalks
and trees or plants and further, into
flowers and fruit and vegetation.
O the innumerable offspring of
your fecund true heart!
Accept, O Earthmother, my
deepest gratitude."

And an amazing fragrance came forth
from where they stood,
and enveloped the gathering,
and everyone knew that Mother Earth
had been deeply moved by those words.

Nikos called out,

"Earthmother, you are my benefactor.
You have offered me magnetism,

electrical energy,
a gravitational tug
to help me release waste matter
and negativities.
You are a power of transformation
to help me alchemize every atomic particle
of food, water, and air so as to benefit every cell
with the nourishment it needs.

"O bless me that I no longer resist you,
but rather assist me as I assist you
to sense in to your centeredness,
to your rhythmic, cyclic, magnetic healing,
and when my time comes
to rest my head, arms, trunk on you,
in the soft caressing bosom of you."

And it seemed that Mother Earth sighed
in quiet acceptance and acquiescence.

Still another named Joshu called out,

"O loving Earthmother mine,
may I cognize from this moment
the capacities of you in me,
your sacred geometry,

crystal-making powers,
an ability to absorb and give forth plenty
and abundance
from a heart of generosity,
from a core of light and space,
at the center of your center.
O Earthmother, I am one with you.
May you be renewed,
as you have renewed me."

And all of a sudden, it seemed everyone had received
a gift—a second set of eyes,
for what they saw was located
deep under the earth—
crystals and diamonds,
octagons and hexagons,
a myriad of mandalas and sparkling designs
in the inner core of Earthmother herself.
And they knew that again,
in her own way,
she had answered them.

Chinda, who had lost her father the year before
and her grandmother ten years before that, offered,

"Mother Earth, you have ever had a magical way

to retain the essence
of everything and everyone that has ever lived,
breathed, spoken, acted,
the way an earthmound or gravestone is able to absorb
the essential love of a loved one
and years later,
when I return to his grave, her grave,
allows me to receive that person's gist,
in a gentle tug at my heart, a timeless greeting.

"You also have a way to empower a land
to retain sacred syllables,
blessings uttered by saints,
ecstatic outcries of pilgrims,
their footprints engraved in the seemingly
self-effacing sand,
their heartprints inscribed indelibly in you,
O Mother mine.
Yes, you hold the secret magic
deep in your down-under,
as mysteriously as megalithic stones
of ancient humankind bear testament
to our ancestry rooted in your powers.
All of these ways of extracting and
retaining quintessentials, O Mother,
attest to your enigmatic yet palpable sanctity."

And this time, an inexplicable breeze wafted across
their faces and brought them an invisible yet
palpable feeling of connectedness, of gratitude.

Now a woman named Devi prayed in this way,

"I am breathing a breath I think of as you, as the earthbreath,
O Mother, and I pray to the heart of you
at the core of your earth,
please cleanse me of all unlovingness,
forgive me for neglecting you,
suffuse me with rootedness,
and help me embody true compassion.
Encourage me to let go of my non-necessities
and receive what is nutritive for my future outpourings
of heart to the cosmos.
May this my prayer be as much for my sake
as for your healing
and for discovering that indeed
you are still whole
even though so much of your body,
from topsoil to mineral depths,
from weather patterns to geological regularities
has been tampered with and disturbed.
May you never be hurt irreparably,

O Mother Earth,
I pray."

And a new sense of compassion was planted
within them,
a sense that they were solidly grounded
in this powerful respect
for their Earthmother.

A poetess among them named Satya uttered this,

"Dear Mother Earth, we barely know you
and the depth of urgings which go on
beneath your muddy hills and plains.
What we see—
arabesques of lemons and limes,
violets and pinks,
greenery and flowery stretching upward
from your roots
inviting sun into the circles
and cycles of your life—
what we feel—
seasonal rhythms and rollings
like waves rising and falling
on the axle of ocean,
thundering its answers

with shafts of wet arrows
or drops of tiptoeing whiteness
or stones hailing response
to your plaintive calls—

"All this and more must tell of a heart
stretched wide
in a sunburst of compassion.
You have paid your toll
in pain and tears.
Please tell us how you feel now,
what message you have for us.

"You speak in signs.
We must learn to read you
or perish."

A hush fell over the whole group huddled there.
Each one dropped into a deep contemplation.
After the long silence, the poetess spoke
what each one longed to say in their hearts,

"Please teach us, O Mother,
through the very earth of our flesh,
the ocean of our waters,
the sun of our fire energy,

the air of our breaths
to listen to your silent throb
and hear your volcanic cry
before mankind carves too deeply
into your softness.
Please teach us to heed you
long before we hurt you
irrevocably,
O Mother Earth."

KA-ELA'S INVITATION

Ka-Ela was thrilled with the beauty in each of the villagers.
They each spoke beyond her imaginings,
and she told them so.

"You are beautiful souls.
Each of you spoke from the exquisite source
deep in your hearts.
I am in awe before your sincerity.
I now suggest that each of us soften our eyes again,
feel the touch beneath our feet,
the contact we have with just the outer skin of Mother Earth,
and ask within our hearts for her to speak to us.
Of course, she has already given
some non-verbal responses
to your hearts' outpourings. Did you notice?"

"Oh yes," several of them acknowledged.

"What did you notice?"

Different people called out,

"A shudder."

"A sigh."

"Tears."

"A fragrance."

"A breeze."

"A vision into the sacred geometry of earth's treasures."

"A feeling of gratitude."

"Yes," Ka-Ela continued.
"You are developing your intuition
and compassion.
Now you are ready to hear her
speak to you her deepest message.
Let each one receive in her or his own way."

And each one felt a stirring,
a sense of emotion, compassion,
receptivity and spaciousness
welling up from within their innermost depths.

EARTHMOTHER'S MESSAGE

And Earthmother began to speak,

"O my children,
here on this sacred mountain,
you have given me great gifts,
feelings of understanding and empathy,
words bearing solace and lovingkindness
and healing.
I feel a lot more energized,
enough to pass an important series
of messages on to you.
Will you listen? Will you receive them
into the innermost abode
in your very own souls?"

Everyone acquiesced in their heart,
and Mother Earth heard their acceptance.

She continued,

"First, I want you to know that children are
the hope of the future.
If you teach them from the start
the true and eternal knowledge
in this universe,
there will be no wars,
no explosions killing your loved ones
and mine,
and there will be no dangerous games of
'my way is better than your way.'
Instead, there will be a new respect,
a new awakening to life's majesty
and mysteries.

"War has no winners.
When people are unable to see
each other's humanness,
they not only destroy each other,
but they destroy me,
what they need to survive,
the gifts of their beautiful earth-garden.

"And thus, I pray that you will allow
your children to trust in their love

for their Earthmother,
to trust in their closeness to land
and sand and ocean
and trees and
to trust in their love for beings of light
and for animals and for all manner
of natural things.

"Above all, teach them the ways
of walking with me,
lightly and with care not to snuff out lives
of green grass or fragile flowers or tiny insects or worms
or ants or other creatures.
Teach them the laws of nature,
to take great care of their bodies,
hearts and souls,
that each align in harmony
with the other
and with all of existence
and in particular, with me.
Let them feel safe to be
the innocent being
each one is."

As she waited for them to drink in this message,
she invited them to drop into the heart of her heart.

She whispered this,

"Let feel the letting down
into where love is,
still in stillness,
intact the touch, purifying,
till the earth refills the well,
fills to fullness,
feels the wellness
full to brim till gentle hands
together heal us full harmonic
once upon a morning shining
we become just what we are
and we are one."

After that poetic utterance,
Ka-Ela became inspired
to exclaim gratefully,

"O thanks be to the axle of goodness
upon which our Mother cranks out
her great stores of grain and seed
and sweetness,
prosperity born of prospering,
goodness born of good-giving,
knowledge born of intelligent knowing

that our good hearts
and our good earth
are interrelated
as each of us turns
upon the axis
of eternal becoming."

It seemed that with each utterance,
each one became ignited with more inspiration
and fullness of heart.

Now Earthmother herself was moved to
reveal yet another secret,

"What you think of as your great world,
is but a miniature of another greater one,
and still of another more vast
and another and another
and all of these unfathomable worlds rest
as do we all
in the arms of the Eternal,
drawing all things into oneness,
catapulting all ripening into fruition
creating of us all
fashioners of ourselves
in the image of love and of light."

Each uplifting statement called forth
spontaneous silence.
And in those moments they were bonded
in a unity which served not only to
raise the awareness
of their collective intelligence
and of their unusual blessings,
but also to bring about healing
for their planetary guardian.

A sense of accelerated ecstasy
began to build itself into the very cells
of their bodies and into the invisibles
surrounding them
and into the spaces within them.
It felt as if this would be the beginning,
the foundation for a new millennium,
the seeding of a new garden
of pure minds and sincere hearts,
here on the flanks
of a distant mountain
of a little known country
of ninety-nine villagers.

Earthmother continued,

"Supporting each other, you help one another evolve,
and as you do this,
you emerge more fully in your own uniqueness.
When you mistakenly perceive each other
to be separate bodies in separate houses
with separate minds and hearts,
you tend to overlook your interconnectedness.
Do not fear losing your true selves;
your uniqueness can never be lost.
Emphasize your common ground
and you will find thousands of gifts."

Everyone sighed with contentment,
for each one felt that Mother Earth
had come back to herself.
She was doing what she does best—
feeding them.
Her food was nourishing their souls.
Her benevolence was awakening their minds.
Her truth was becoming embodied
in their bodies.

"Now, I offer you a challenge,"
Mother Earth continued.

"If you were to think with the Mind
of the universe,
what thoughts would you have?
If you were to feel with the Heart
of the universe,
what feelings would you have?
If you were to feel your body to be
an extension of my body and to feel that body
to be an extension of the cosmos—
the waters, sun, wind, air, the ethers,
stars, moons, galaxies, all of space,
how would you act? What would you do?
How would your lives be different?"

BECOMING A COSMIC BEING

Everyone was struck by the power
in Earthmother's questions.
Each one took to heart and accepted
her challenge
to expand beyond anything
they had ever before conceived of.
By now, each wanted more for themselves,
more for each other,
more for their planet.

Ka-Ela felt the energy and suggested again
that they close their eyes
and inquire within themselves
and at the same time,
realize with a special awareness
that everyone else
was asking themselves these questions
at the very same moment.

In this way, she asked,

"Can you sense that you are indeed thinking
with one mind,
feeling with one heart?

"And when you feel touched by a response,
call it out! One word or many, it does not matter."

Satya began,

"Magnanimity! With a cosmic heart, I would
be enormously generous!"

Helena continued,

"Yes! Largesse of heart! I have always wanted
a heart so spacious that it could hold the entire world."

Next Eli spoke out,

"Vastness of scope! I would be able to see
with limitless vision all of the universe at once
and instead of limited views,
I would have an omniversal view,
seeing all points of view simultaneously."

Maitri continued his thought,

"And that kind of vision would be
matched by fair-mindedness,
an egalitarian attitude, free from prejudice
against anyone for any reason."

Devi added,

"And matching that would be a profound sense
of equanimity, of balance,
and undisturbed inner space."

Next Nikos said,

"Because of that equanimity,
we would be kind, loving, and inspired
to regard everyone with unconditional acceptance."

Then Eli added,

"And with unconditional acceptance,
would that not lead to dramatic responsiveness?
Acts of compassion?"

Lastly, Ka-Ela asserted,

"And the more we think, feel, and live
in this cosmic, responsive, unlimited way,
the more our good becomes magnified,
and the more magnitude
to our good,
the more magnetism in our bodies,
minds, and hearts.
Everything leads to wondrous and sparkling health
and wholeness, and as such, imagine who benefits?
Remember our original mission?"

"Yes," everyone agreed. "We would be able
in these ways to restore Mother Earth
to her original wholeness.
We would be the co-creators with
the Universe, with the Goddess,
with...."

All of a sudden, they realized that
Ka-Ela was representing this very One
and Only Being, the Goddess.

She read their thoughts and said,

"No, I am not the One you think I am.
Only if you recognize that you are
as much the One as I,
then together, as a manifestation of
the cosmic Mind-Heart,
we birth the One into this world
again and again,
in ever new and creative fashion."

COSMIC EMBODIMENT

Ka-Ela brought momentum to this idea.

"Friends, we have inspired one another,
we have become more fully ourselves as individuals
and more united with one another.
It is as if we are becoming one big Mind
and one big Heart.
Now it is time to gather our unified energy
and flow with it.
We can move down the mountain
to an open place in your village,
and with grace and gratitude for this blessing of our unity,
move with our energy, flow and dance together."

One villager named Shanta asked,

"What do you mean?

"We do not know how to do that."

Ka-Ela suggested,

"Let us see what transpires once we form a circle
at the base of the mountain.
Perhaps you will be surprised at how you move.

"Your mind does not have to know anything.
Just let your body move.
This heaven we have just shared
is now to be embodied
in our earth-bodies, on our earth.
Come, let us begin.
Walk, run, or flow down the mountain paths as a
running stream or as a rainbow of colors or as a
shaft of sunlight.
Experiment! Be free!"

And with that permission
to be free and to move in the image
of a light or a color or a flow of water,
the villagers ran down the mountain.
If anyone had been looking from afar
it would have seemed that what descended that mountain
was a watery flow, or a flash of floating colors

and arrows of light.
That person would also have heard
squeals of delight and laughter
like the sounds of innocent children.

Once gathered at the base of the mountain,
in the large circle surrounded by trees
where the village elders used to confer on various issues,
the villagers began to hum.
Each one's hum harmonized with the other's,
and soon, without needing to wait for instructions,
they began to sway their bodies
to the songs they were creating together.
They half-closed their eyes and attuned themselves
to their deeper energies
which this morning of sharing
had awakened in them,
and a continuity of ecstasy
and centeredness unfolded
well into the afternoon.

Ka-Ela floated off to a high cliff
without being noticed by the group.
From afar, what she observed amazed
and delighted her.
At times, each person resembled a flower,

unfolding from bud to full opening.
At others, each became an element—
a flowing river, an ecstatic wind,
a gentle rain, a radiant sun,
even an emergent butterfly.
From afar, the circle looked like a vast mandala,
a design of perfect geometry.

Satya suggested,

"I feel so peaceful.
And everyone looks so harmonious
and beatific, I wish that we could travel
round the world with this gift."

"What do you mean?
What gift?" Shanta asked.

"To offer to the world
the peace and friendship and harmony
we have just been creating," Satya answered.

"Yes," said Eli,
"dancing in this joyful yet concentrated way
is a way to bring others to contentment, awareness,
and peace.

"We could create circle dances
and invite the peoples of the world to join us.
This could be our peace embodiment."

And they turned to look for Ka-Ela.
At first they could not find her.
She laughed and they heard her laughter,
but still she was nowhere to be found.

"Where are you, Ka-Ela? We need you,"
they called out.

CONSCIOUS ATTUNEMENT

Ka-Ela had made herSelf invisible
but could be heard when she sang out,

"Your vision is a good one.
Now you sit quietly where you are,
upon this circle of harmonious dance,
and ask yourselves the questions you wish to ask of me.
This will begin your journey toward the One,
the perfection within you,
who knows what you want to know,
who can be trusted, who can guide you,
individually and together.
Above all, let this sitting
in quiet receptivity and inner harmony
be your daily attunement."

Eli asked her,

"What do you mean by attunement?"

Ka-Ela responded,

"A harmonious feeling of alignment
with your highest good,
with what corresponds to your deepest longing
and creative wellspring,
and the discovery that what is healing and joyful for you
is also for the well-being of the entire cosmos."

Now each villager was inspired
to turn within and tune into an inner mystery.
Ka-Ela had taken them into a new level of understanding.
They had resonated with their Earthmother
and dedicated themselves to her healing.
Now they realized that
in order to continue the cosmic flow,
they had to attune to themselves and to their own meaning,
their own gifts, their personally refined sensibilities,
with reliance not on Ka-Ela
and not on concepts,
but instead on inner resonances
and conscious attunements.

The villagers grew very quiet.

The village elder, Tzaddik, suggested,
"Let us designate a portion of each day as a sacred time for ourselves.
Let us sit together, each of us conscious of breathing
with awareness,
each of us asking our hearts to tell us what is true
in the most honest way possible.
Let us notice what arises,
whether it be painful or pleasurable,
sensing its texture, its color, its depth, its message
without riding on any highs or lows,
but let this be our daily work—
to cleanse and honor
the earth each of us is made of,
and then what a blessing
we will be in this world!"

And it was so.
At dusk that evening, the villagers gathered.
While watching the sun disappear from the vast horizon,
as if dropping into Mother Earth,
each one dropped into a heart-space inside
to commune and ask for what is true and real
and most meaningful to reveal itself.

Just at the close of their sitting,
a most unusual phenomenon occurred.

A murmuring.
A joining of voices in prayer.
And the discovery that in each one's heart,
these words arose,

"O Cosmic One, the very source and fiber
of existence,
Creator of love, harmony, and beauty,
open us to Your guidance
which appears both within and without,
reveal to us that which is hidden
and beautiful and mysterious
so that we do not miss the meaning
of our precious human life,
so that we come to cherish each life
as truly as our own.

"Most revered Essence of all substances,
transform us while we sleep,
teach us while we dream,
open our vision to the reality
and truth behind our layers of embodiment,
and unite us all in loving being."

As they opened their eyes,
they realized their village had become unified,

their vision was encompassing each other
and the whole planet,
their hearts were soft and tender,
and their minds expanded.
They felt inspired to live lovingly,
and as harmlessly as possible in the time they would have
on this plane of earthly existence.

DREAM-HEALING

That night
the ninety-nine villagers experienced sleep
as a new form of receiving and giving.
While Ka-Ela slept her dreamless sleep
complete in its restfulness and easeful in its transmission
of rays of healing wisdom from the core of her heart,
the newly inspired minds of the people created many-faceted dreams,
the way a kaleidoscope creates ever-shifting designs.

Some walked upon a golden thread
which served as a continually lengthening highway
to reach into distant lands and suffering hearts.
They did not interfere in anyone's free choice
or personal space,
but they stretched out their arms to offer love and blessings
and well-wishing.
Others recited their prayers as they walked or flew,
with the help of their golden threads,

to bring peace to the distressed,
to share healing with the diseased,
to awaken insight in the confused.

Ka-Ela sighed with contentment,

"Now you have risen to the height
of beings of light.
You are my peers, my helpers,
my co-workers, for as your bodies sleep
and dream, you release your energies
for the benefit of the world.
I am indeed deeply gratified.
And by day, as you awaken, you shall soon discover
your unique purpose."

AWAKENING TO DAWN

Each one awoke,
some with the memory of their amazing journeys
into other lands and lives,
some with just a feeling of satisfaction
that somehow he or she had given a gift to someone
in the night while seemingly just sleeping.

Again, they gathered in the village circle
which they had selected as the place to sit together
in silence, meditation, prayer, and dance
at dawn and at dusk.
As the light streamed forth in thick, white sheaths
from behind snow-capped peaks and valleys to the east,
each one felt the rising of the dawn within.

A unifying hum arose spontaneously
from the back of their throats,
and Ka-Ela could hear from her distant peak

the profound vibrations of a unifying sound
resounding for miles and miles.

And not only could she hear it,
but with her omni-seeing eyes,
she watched the sounds travel
round the planet and realized that even though
the majority of the world was caught in webs of affliction
and conflict from which they could not
extricate themselves,
their consciousness could be touched
by the intensity of love and kindness
and prayer offered sincerely
by individuals and groups like this one
concentrating on global well-being
and planetary healing.

As if reading her thoughts,
the villagers joined in this,

"Let us bring all of our minds together
as one so as to potentiate our intentions."

Helena asked,

"What are our intentions? Let us name them!

"Let everyone speak, one by one!"

"To transform attitudes of uncaring to caring!"

"To offset acts of violence with acts of love and respect!"

"To inspire human hearts in despair or rage to see
their own self-worth
so that they won't have to throw their frustrations
onto Mother Earth or onto their fellow beings!"

"To create a new vision —
of everyone as friends sharing a common source,
instead of as enemies vying with one another for supremacy."

"To lift the consciousness of humanity to the awareness
that everyone belongs to one family of humankind."

"And that everyone belongs to another family as well,
a divine family that is of the same light and love
that Ka-Ela emanates."

Ka-Ela heard them and exclaimed,

"Yes, each of you, as well as me,
we are beings of cosmic love and vast, far-reaching light.

"We can hold in our hearts everyone everywhere,
even the whole universe.
The space in our hearts is not limited by our skin and bones.
The space in our hearts is able to contain the entirety of life,
and that is why we are here,
meditating, singing, dancing, praying
for all beings and their well-being.
May it be as we intend."

Now that it was dawn,
and Ka-Ela's message and their own intentions
had entered into the depths of their being,
they erupted in passionate song,

"O Cosmic One in whom we all live and have our being,
help us to mirror You,
to broaden our minds and open our hearts,
to allow others to blossom
in the light of our acceptance
and affirmation of life and love.
Please guide us in facing
any traces of bias, resentment, insecurity, and
arrogance in ourselves
before any of these erupt to fuel acts
of destructiveness and pain.

"We want to be able to hold ourselves
in our own embrace.
Help us to be present to the Presence
as it arises in us moment by moment."

HIGH NOONTIME

All morning long,
Ka-Ela watched the unfolding of the villagers' goodness
in the loving words they spoke to each other,
in the sweet ways they taught school to their children,
in the multiple activities they engaged in
to care for Mother Earth.
The primary work was to prepare and sow seeds in the earth.

Before choosing a site, they communed with Earthmother
and also with the seeds.
From each, they found out the ideal place to turn over the soil
and the right spot to plant each seed.
They communed with the sun whom they called father
and with rain and wind whom they called sister and brother
and with the ethers whom they called angels
so that each harmonized with the other
and each provided that which was needed
the moment it was required.

They sowed barley and rice, millet and wheat,
quinoa and spelt,
aduki beans and lentils, green beans and mung,
acorn squash and pumpkin,
beets and carrots, kale and onions,
chard and spinach, romaine and arugula.
And Mother Earth sighed with relief
to have such careful gardeners.
She could relax and trust that they would take care
not to act hastily or carelessly,
but rather to act with caring and conscious intention
to be ever a blessing to both Earthmother and themselves.

At noontime, they ceased from their labors
and gathered upon the village circle to eat the fruit of their labor and
first, to give thanks and praise
to the Being out of whom Earthmother issued forth,
out of whom seeds were sprung,
out of whom the elements arose,
out of whom their own goodness
was birthed.

"O great Source of our life,
of our minds and hearts and limbs,
of our goodness and kindness and truth,

of our inspired intentions and actions,
of our insights and visions,
of our expressions in words and dance,
of our radiance and gift-giving and love,
thanks be for Your blessings.
May we remain ever aligned with
our highest purpose.
May we stay open to Your guidance
toward the cosmic good,
toward what facilitates our transformation,
toward the manifestation of our divine inheritance
which is the seed You have planted within us
as a blessing and a covenant
with us for all time.
May we hear Your voice within our own
and feel Your presence within us."

KA-ELA'S DEPARTURE

Ka-Ela was nearly speechless with gratitude and wonder
at the transformation
in this village of ninety-nine persons.
She felt the shift in each one
to become Cosmic-conscious,
a being of Light
ready to live in the heart
of what is true and real and beneficial
and to shine that light upon the world
by day or by night
so that others would be inspired
to begin their journey toward the true life,
the examined life,
the life which sees itself
as an extension of one Being
and experiences and acknowledges its value.

She reappeared in their midst,

and spoke to them from a hillside
a few kilometers away.

"Friends,
I am deeply moved by your wondrous changes.
You have risen to heights and dropped into depths
of soul understandings
and clear realizations.
You are well on the way to seeing your true selves.
There is no greater work in the world
than this —
to see and appreciate and value your priceless value,
your diamond-like essence,
your radiant potentials,
your wellspring of ever-renewing resources
of love, light, life, and infinite divine qualities.

"I am so confident in your capacity to take yourselves further
into your individual and collective journeys
that I have decided to leave you now
and travel to other parts of your planet.
I believe you will understand my decision,
for it is my mission and it is for you
to continue to discover yours,
as together, wherever we are,
we honor our Earthmother

and live in such a way as to give her reverence,
just as we have been practicing
with one another here on this mountain.
May we continue to uncover more and more living layers
of the message of love in our time."

The villagers took in what Ka-Ela shared
about her forthcoming journey.
Helena, Satya, Nikos, Maitri, Eli, Shanta,
and many others shed tears as they spoke,

"O Ka-Ela, we will miss you.
We barely feel ready to be on our own.
But we understand that
others are calling out for you,
and Mother Earth needs you to give your message
to other peoples in other lands.
We will not cease to do our inner work,
tending our inner qualities,
the seeds implanted within our souls
that we may manifest our true selves
while on this earth,
for the sake of our divine embodiment
and for the sake of peace on earth."

"Thank you, my beloved friends,

and please know that I shall not be far.
You can contact me in your hearts
and have a conversation with me
anywhere at anytime,
but best of all,
commune with the Source
within your own hearts and souls.
That Source will never fail you.
And we will be engaged
in the work of the message of love
for all time."

"Godspeed," called out Tzaddik.
"Godspeed, godspeed, godspseed," echoed
through the gathering.

And Eli jumped up,

"Wait, Ka-Ela, you forgot someone.
Let us hear once more from Mother Earth.
After all, it was she who invited you here.
Now let us allow her the last word."

Ka-Ela smiled,

"You are right. I agree. Now you can call out

and ask Mother Earth to speak again, if she chooses."

Eli asked the villagers to join hands in a circle.

Then Satya offered,

"Let us invite Mother Earth's blessing
upon Ka-Ela for her work and for ours."

In silence, they closed their eyes lightly, as they had been taught,
and dropped gently into their heart-space.
Then, each in her and his own way invited
Earthmother to respond.
Each remained open and attentive and listening.

In a few minutes,
a breeze stirred, a fragrance wafted through them,
and the space within them opened and reverberated
with these words,

"I am here,
Earthmother is here with each of you,
mindful of how you have dedicated yourselves
to cleansing your minds and hearts,
and how in so doing,
you have cleansed the atmosphere

in which I dwell.
And your well-wishings, pure intentions,
and inspiring actions have brought about a great feeling
of well-being and healing to my poor struggling soul.

"Now that the work has begun in this corner of my earthen body,
now I feel sure that it will continue.
And the momentum of your enthusiasm
has ignited mine. I am feeling better and better!

"To Ka-Ela,
I offer my deepest gratitude
for answering instantaneously my desperate prayer.
You are truly an angel of the Divine, for
'ka' means like,
and 'ela' means goddess.
Like unto the Goddess, the Source
of our existence, you are, and
may your living in that awareness
and in that awesome response-ability bear great fruit
and great blessings
for all of your divine endeavors.

"I am inspired to bring forth as much nourishment
as I ever could before I felt overpowered
by the forces of darkness.

"Now I feel our collective power
and with the realization of our oneness,
there is nothing we cannot face,
nothing we cannot journey into.

"May we all feel the blessings
of who and what we really are,
shining drops in the eternal sea,
radiant stars in the infinite sky,
sparkling gems in the divine mine,
rays of light in the forever sun,
magnets in the magnetic field,
the dust out of which existence is made,
the core and essence of all reality.
Bless you, Ka-Ela!
Bless you, sister and brother earth-beings!"

"Bless you, Earthmother!
We are one!
We are one with the One!
We will journey together!
Godspeed!"

And throughout the cosmos for those with ears to hear,
"GODSPEED" resounded
for countless eons and future generations

as a blessing from this time
and a promise for all time.

CLARE ROSENFIELD

Clare Rosenfield, also known as Satya-Jai (meaning Essence or Truth of the Heart), is a poet, artist, writer, meditation teacher, harpist, healer, and licensed clinical social worker who has founded a holistic approach to self-healing called Contact Healing™.

A Smith College graduate and former French teacher in Boston, Lagos, Bangkok, and New York, Clare received both her M.A. in French and later an M.S. degree in Social Work from Columbia University.

Drawing on more than fifty years of experience integrating therapeutic approaches from East and West, she empowers people with healing meditations, breathing experiments, inner journeys, and the cultivation of compassion towards oneself and all of life. Through her work as Director of the Global Healing Foundation (**www.globalhealingfoundation.org**), she is committed to healing the planet through helping indigenous Colombian healers protect their sacred lands, as well as through global healing meditations, soothing harp-playing, writings and poetry.

She has illustrated nearly all of her poetry collections, verse narratives, and children's stories with watercolors, pastels, acrylics, Touch Drawings, or charcoal.

To invite Clare for readings, to schedule individual sessions, or to place orders for her books and paintings, contact: **crosenfield9@gmail.com** and **www.contacthealing.com.**

OTHER PUBLICATIONS BY CLARE ROSENFIELD

BOOKS

Ten Lives of the Buddha: Siamese Temple Paintings and Jataka Tales
by Elizabeth Wray, Clare Rosenfield, and Dorothy Bailey (1972)

Reverence For All Life And Vegetarianism
by Clare Rosenfield and Linda Segall (1979)

Twelve Facets of Reality: The Jain Path to Freedom
by Gurudev Shree Chirabhanu, edited by Clare Rosenfield (1980)

Gurudev Shree Chitrabhanu: A Man With A Vision
by Clare Rosenfield (1982)

To Light One Candle: Universal Prayers For Peace
by Clare Rosenfield and Pramoda Chitrabhanu (1990, revised 1993)

POETRY COLLECTIONS & VERSE NARRATIVES

dance upon the winds swept cloudless (1987)

Seasonals (1991)

Roll On Great Earth (2002)

The Call of Mother Earth: How a Being of Light Draws Forth Humanity's Response (2004, 2017, third printing 2021)

Tall Grasses of Woods Hole & Other Summery Poems (2004)

Nameless One of Splendor: Her Sacred Arts of Creation (2005)

Ninsun: Wise Mother of Gilgamesh (2012)

Your Inmost Tree of Life: An Invitation (2015)

SUN-CHILD (2017, second edition 2021)

Seven Meditations for Children (2017, second edition 2021)

The Little Girl Who Wanted to be a Tree (in press, 2021)

To the Rescue: Little Creatures, How Do I Love Thee (in press, 2021)

ARTICLES

"The Mythical Animal Statues at the Prasat Phratheppabidon" in *In Memoriam Phya Anuman Rajadhon* (1970)

"Birds Of A Feather" in *Sawaddi* (1970)

"The World Of The Buddha At Sanchi" in *Sawaddi* (1973)

"The Zigzag Line in Siamese Temple Painting" in *Sawaddi* (1973)

"If the Animals Could Speak" in *Vegetarian Voice* (1981)

"Be Stirred By a Lob-Ster" in *Vegetarian Voice* (1982)

"STOP—and Meditate" in *The Greenburgh Inquirer* (1983)

"The Power of Thought" in *Inner Voice* (2003)

"Our Kaleidoscopic Reality" in *Inner Voice* (2003)

"Breaking the Cycle of Self-Sabotaging Thoughts" in *Inner Voice* (2003)

www.ingramcontent.com/pod-product-compliance
Lightning Source LLC
LaVergne TN
LVHW041649060526
838200LV00040B/1776